SLOW COOKER COOKBOOK FOR TWO

EASY AND DELICIOUS READY-TO-EAT MEALS
SLOW COOKER RECIPES **FOR TWO**

Copyright © 2017 Dana Summers
All rights reserved.

Published by The Fruitful Mind LTD.

DISCLAIMER

All rights Reserved. No part of this publication or the information in it may be quoted from or reproduced in any form by means such as printing, scanning, photocopying or otherwise without prior written permission of the copyright holder.

Disclaimer and Terms of Use: Effort has been made to ensure that the information in this book is accurate and complete, however, the author and the publisher do not warrant the accuracy of the information, text and graphics contained within the book due to the rapidly changing nature of science, research, known and unknown facts and internet. The Author and the publisher do not hold any responsibility for errors, omissions or contrary interpretation of the subject matter herein. This book is presented solely for motivational and informational purposes only.

Special Gifts For Readers

As a reader of this book, you can get free access to other bonuses from The Fruitful Mind, including:
- 40 Healthy Habits Wellness Guide
- Fast Metabolism Secrets PDF Report
- **Free & Discounted #1 Bestselling Health eBooks**

And much more that will help you lose weight, increase energy and feel great! To get these free bonuses, please visit:

www.thefruitfulmind.com

Introduction

Is your refrigerator stocked with leftovers you'll never eat? Slowly, yet surely, your Tupperware containers fill up, grow moldy, and then cause you enormous guilt as you toss tons of once-vibrant vegetables and meats down the garbage can. You're an empty nester, you're just a couple, you're a busy professional—or you're single—and you can't handle these 8- or 10-serving recipes any longer. It's just wasteful.

In this Slow Cooker Cookbook for Two, I offer simple recipes; ones that help you toss everything into the slow cooker in the morning, and forget about the recipe till night, when you can dive in and eat up! Each recipe offers wholesome ingredients, with vegetables and meats and spices that will rev your metabolism, lending all the appropriate proteins, carbs, and healthy fats to keep you rolling along in your busy lifestyle. The recipes don't include preservative-rich ingredients, which ultimately cause inflammation and increased fatigue (not to mention weight gain). And they're about a million times better than any fast food diet you might necessarily pick up, due to time constraints.

With each dish, from the wholesome breakfast recipes, to the soups, stews, and chilies, to the chicken, seafood, beef, pork, vegetarian, and even dessert recipes, I include the preparation time, which normally allows you to set the slow cooker and then forget about it, immediately. Your long days of hovering over the stove are over. Armed with your slow cooker, and this cookbook, you can lose weight, improve your stamina, and bolster your happy way of life.

Table of Contents

INTRODUCTION 5
SLOW COOKER BREAKFASTS FOR TWO 11
Slow Cooker Huevos Rancheros for Two .. 12
Quinoa with Cranberry and Coconut 14
Mediterranean Egg Dish for Two 15
Granola Apple Crumble for Breakfast 17

SLOW COOKER SOUPS, STEWS, AND CHILIES FOR TWO 19
Nutritious and Soul-Warming Turkey Chili 20
Asian Spiced Beef Curry Soup 22
Split Pea and Turkey Soup 25
Black Bean Soup 27
South of the Border Chicken Taco Soup 30
Louisiana Jambalaya 32
Red Potato Stew 34
Ground Beef "Hamburger" Stew 36
Vegetarian's Delight Chili 38
Ham and Lentil Soup 40
Wintertime Zucchini and Italian Sausage Soup 42
Mother's Best Chicken Noodle Soup 44
Mushroom and Chicken Stew 46

SLOW COOKER SEAFOOD AND CHICKEN RECIPES FOR TWO 49
Lime and Cilantro Chicken 50
Slow Cooked BBQ Chicken................................ 51
Southerner's Chicken Creole 53
Garlic and Honey Chicken 55
Asian Tang Chicken... 57
Chicken Adobo 59
Italian Chicken Cacciatore 60
Cheesy Cheddar Chicken 61

AFRICAN MARRAKESH CHICKEN 63
SOUTH AMERICAN SPICED CHICKEN 65
CHICKEN FROM THAILAND 67
FRENCH CHICKEN COOKED WITH WHITE WINE ... 69
CRAB AND SPINACH ALFREDO LASAGNA 71
SALMON CASSEROLE 73
SOUTH AMERICAN TILAPIA 75

SLOW COOKER BEEF AND PORK RECIPES FOR TWO 77

CHICAGO'S FAVORITE ITALIAN BEEF 78
3-INGREDIENT BUTTER BEEF 79
MEXICAN-STYLE BEEF BARBACOA 80
A TRI-TIP BEEF LOIN ROAST 82
EASTERN ASIA BEEF TACOS 84
TOP TASTE BEEF BRISKET 86
SLOW COOKED BBQ BEER BEEF 89
ITALIAN PORK CACCIATORE 92
MEXICAN PORK "CARNITAS" 94
TWO-INGREDIENT SAUERKRAUT PORK 96
ULTIMATE TENDER PORK ROAST 97
SUPER-SIMPLE BBQ PORK 98
PUERTO RICAN PORK 99
SUPER PICANTE PORK 101

SLOW COOKER VEGETARIAN RECIPES FOR TWO 103

EGGPLANT PARMESAN FOR TWO 104
GREEK'S EGGPLANT AND SQUASH STEW 106
SLOW COOKED LENTILS AND BARLEY 108
CRANBERRY, APPLE, AND SQUASH DISH 110
VEGETARIAN CURRY WITH INDIAN SPICES 111
PARSNIP, TURNIP AND CARROT TAGINE 113
SPINACH AND PUMPKIN CHILI 115
VEGGIE-FRIENDLY BUFFALO DIP 117
CHEESY AND BUTTERY SQUASH 118
SPLIT BLACK LENTILS WITH CURRY 120
RICE AND MUSHROOM CASSEROLE 122

SLOW COOKED ARTICHOKE DIP 124
VEGETARIAN MINESTRONE 126
VEGAN JAMBALAYA 128

SLOW COOKER DESSERT RECIPES FOR TWO
.... **131**
PUMPKIN PIE SPICED APPLE SAUCE 132
SLOW COOKED TAPIOCA PUDDING 133
GRANDMA'S BEST CHOCOLATE CAKE 134
PEACH COBBLER 136
CONCLUSION 138

SLOW COOKER BREAKFAST FOR TWO

w Cooker Huevos ancheros for Two

Recipe Makes 2 Servings.

Preparation Time: 2 hours and 15 minutes

Ingredients:

- 3 eggs
- ¼ cup half-and-half
- 3 ounces Monterey Jack, shredded
- 1 minced garlic clove
- ¼ tsp. ancho chili powder
- ½ tsp. black pepper
- 1 ounce green chilies, chopped
- 2 corn tortillas
- 2 ounces taco sauce
- Avocado, cilantro, and lime for garnish and to taste

Directions:

First, spray the interior of your slow cooking spray.

Next, beat together the eggs with the half-and-half, along with half of the Monterey Jack cheese, pepper, garlic, chilies and the chili powder. Pour this mixture into the slow cooker, and then cook on low, covered, for two hours.

At this time, remove the lid from the slow cooker, and then pour the taco sauce over the eggs. Cover the eggs completely, using a spoon, and then add the rest of the cheese over the eggs. Return the lid to the slow cooker, and then continue to cook the eggs for 15 minutes more.

Next, allow the mixture to cool. Slice the eggs into wedges, and then serve the eggs over tortillas. Garnish with avocadoes, cilantro, and lime, and enjoy.

Quinoa with Cranberry and Coconut

Recipe Makes 2 Servings.

Preparation Time: 4 hours

Ingredients:

- ¾ cup dried quinoa
- ½ cup coconut water
- ¼ cup cranberries, dried
- 2 tsp. honey
- 1 tsp. vanilla
- ¼ cup sliced almonds
- ¼ cup coconut, dried

Directions:

Add the above ingredients to a slow cooker and cook on low for four hours. Afterwards, stir well, and serve. Enjoy.

Mediterranean Egg Dish for Two

Recipe Makes 2 Servings.

Preparation Time: 5 hours and 10 minutes

Ingredients:

- 3 eggs
- ¼ cup milk
- ½ tsp. salt
- ½ tbsp. diced red onion
- 1 minced garlic clove
- 1 tsp. pepper
- ¼ cup diced sundried tomatoes
- 1 cup spinach
- ¼ cup sliced mushrooms
- 1/8 cup feta cheese, crumbled

Directions:

First, stir together the milk, eggs, salt, and pepper in a medium-sized bowl.

Add the onion and the garlic at this time. Stir well.

Next, add the spinach, mushrooms, and the sundried tomatoes, and pour the mixture into the slow cooker.

Top the mixture with the feta cheese crumbles, and then cook the mixture on low for five hours.

At this time, serve the eggs warm, and enjoy.

Granola Apple Crumble for Breakfast

Recipe Makes 2 Servings.

Preparation Time: 4 hours

Ingredients:

- 1 granny smith apple
- 1 tbsp. butter
- 1 tbsp. maple syrup
- ½ cup granola cereal
- ½ tsp. cinnamon
- 1/8 cup apple juice
- ¼ tsp. nutmeg, ground

Directions:

First, core, peel and slice the apples.

Add the apples, butter, maple syrup, granola, cinnamon, apple juice, and the nutmeg to the slow cooker, and stir well.

Cook the ingredients on low for four hours, stirring occasionally.

Afterwards, stir well, and serve warm or cold. Enjoy.

SLOW COOKER
SOUPS, STEWS, AND 'CHILIES'
FOR TWO

Nutritious and Soul-Warming Turkey Chili

Recipe Makes 4 Servings.

Preparation Time: 7 hours

Ingredients:

- ½ tbsp. olive oil
- ½ pound ground turkey
- 15 ounces kidney beans
- 10 ounces tomato soup, low sodium
- ¼ onion, diced
- 7 ounces black beans
- 1 tbsp. chili beans
- ½ tsp. red pepper flakes
- 2 tsp. garlic powder
- ¼ tsp. cumin, ground
- ½ tsp. allspice
- ½ tsp. pepper
- ½ tsp. salt

Directions:

First, add the olive oil to a medium-sized skillet, and cook the turkey in the oil over medium heat until browned.

Next, spray the interior of a slow cooker with cooking spray, and add the turkey, beans, tomato soup, and the onion to the slow cooker.

Stir well, and then season with red pepper flakes, chili powder, cumin, garlic powder, allspice, black pepper, and salt. Stir well.

Next, cover the slow cooker, and cook on low for seven hours. Stir well, and serve warm. Enjoy.

Asian Spiced Beef Curry Soup

Recipe Makes 4 Servings.

Preparation Time: 7 hours and 30 minutes

Ingredients:

- 2 tbsp. olive oil
- ½ onion, diced
- 3 green chili peppers, sliced
- 4 minced garlic cloves
- 1 tsp. ginger paste
- 2 cardamom seeds, whole
- 1 clove, whole
- 1 tsp. cumin
- 1 tsp. coriander
- 1 tsp. garlic powder
- ½ tsp. cayenne powder
- 1 cinnamon stick
- ½ cup water

- 1 ¼ pound beef chunk, sliced into one-inch pieces

Directions:

First, add the olive oil to a medium-sized skillet, and then add the onion. Cook over medium heat until the onion is clear. This should take about five minutes.

Next, add the green chilies, garlic, ginger paste, clove, cardamom seeds, and the cinnamon stick. Cook until the garlic browns, which should take an additional five more minutes.

Next, add the spices: garlic powder, cumin, coriander, and the cayenne pepper. Add the water at this time, and then stir well. Cook for three minutes, and then pour this mixture into the slow cooker.

Add the beef to the slow cooker, stir well, and then cover the slow cooker.

Cook on LOW for seven hours, or until the beef is cooked all the way through. Serve warm, and enjoy.

Split Pea and Turkey Soup

Recipe Makes 4 Servings.

Preparation Time: 5 hours

Ingredients:

- ½ pound split peas, dried
- 1 cup water
- 1½ pound smoked turkey, diced
- 1 cup chopped carrot
- 1½ cups chicken broth
- ¾ cup chopped celery
- ½ tsp. garlic powder
- ½ chopped onion
- ¼ tsp. oregano
- ¼ tsp. garlic powder
- 1 bay leaf

Directions:

First, stir together the split peas, water, smoked turkey, carrot, chicken broth, celery, garlic powder, onion, oregano, garlic powder, and the bay leaf in a slow cooker.

Stir well, and then cook the soup on high for five hours.

Before serving, throw away the bay leaf, and enjoy.

Black Bean Soup

Recipe Makes 4 Servings.

Preparation Time: 7 hours and 20 minutes

Ingredients:

- 2 cups water
- 6 ounces black beans, dried
- ½ carrot, chopped
- ½ chopped stalk of celery
- ½ diced red onion
- 14 ounces peeled and diced tomatoes
- ½ diced jalapeno pepper
- ½ diced green pepper
- 2 tbsp. dried lentils
- 1 tsp. salt
- 1 tbsp. red wine vinegar
- ½ tsp. black pepper
- ¼ tsp. oregano, dried
- 1 tsp. cumin
- 3 tbsp. white rice

Directions:

First, add the beans to a medium-sized saucepan, and add the water to the beans. Stir well, and bring the pot of beans and water to a boil over medium-high heat for 10 minutes.

After 10 minutes, cover the pot and remove the beans from the heat. Allow them to stand, covered, for one hour. Drain them and rinse them at this time.

Next, add the beans to a slow cooker. Add another cup of water. Cover the slow cooker and cook on HIGH for three hours.

Afterwards, add the vegetables to the soup, along with the rest of the ingredients. Stir well, cover, and cook the soup on LOW for three hours.

With 20 minutes left of cook time, add the rice to the slow cooker, and stir well.

After the soup's done cooking, add half of the soup to a blender and puree it until smooth. Pour the mixture back into the slow cooker, and serve warm.

South of the Border Chicken Taco Soup

Recipe Makes 4 Servings.

Preparation Time: 7 hours

Ingredients:

- ½ chopped onion
- 7 ounces black beans
- 8 ounces chili beans
- 7 ounces corn
- 4 ounces tomato sauce
- 5 ounces diced tomatoes
- 6 ounces beer
- ½ package taco seasoning
- 5 ounces green chilies
- 1 boneless chicken breast
- 4 ounces shredded cheddar cheese

Directions:

First, add the onion, beans, corn, beer, tomato sauce, and tomatoes to a slow cooker. Stir well, and then add the taco seasoning. Stir once more.

Next, place the chicken over the ingredients, pressing down on it to cover it with the other ingredients.

Cook the chicken and mixture on low heat, covered, for five hours.

After five hours, remove the chicken from the slow cooker, and then allow it to cool. Shred the chicken, and then place the chicken back in the slow cooker.

Cook for an additional two hours at this time, and then coat the soup with cheddar cheese and green chilies. Serve warm, and enjoy.

Louisiana Jambalaya

Recipe Makes 4 Servings

Preparation Time: 8 hours

Ingredients:

- 5 ounces chicken, cubed
- 14 ounces diced tomatoes, with juice from can
- 5 ounces sliced sausage
- ½ chopped green pepper
- ½ chopped onion
- 1/3 cup chopped celery
- 1/3 cup chicken broth
- 1 tsp. oregano
- 1 tsp. parsley
- 1 tsp. Cajun seasoning
- ½ tsp. cayenne pepper
- ¼ tsp. dried thyme
- 6 ounces frozen, already cooked shrimp, no tails or veins

Directions:

First, add the chicken, sausage, tomatoes, onion, celery, green pepper, and the broth to a slow cooker. Season the mixture with the spices, and stir well.

Next, cover the mixture, and cook on low for eight hours. With 30 minutes left, add the shrimp to the slow cooker, and stir well.

Serve the jambalaya warm, and enjoy.

Red Potato Stew

Recipe Makes 4 Servings

Preparation Time: 9 hours and 20 minutes

Ingredients:

- 10 cubed red potatoes
- 1 cup bacon bits
- 2 tbsp. flour
- 1 minced garlic clove
- 1 diced onion, red
- 2 tbsp. chicken bouillon
- 1 tbsp. ranch dressing
- 1 tsp. salt
- 1 tsp. parsley, dried
- ½ tsp. pepper
- 2 ½ cups water
- ¾ cup half-and-half
- ¾ cup shredded cheddar cheese

Directions:

First, place the potatoes in the very bottom of your slow cooker, scattering them over the expanse of the bottom. Add the flour over the potatoes, and then toss the potatoes to coat them in the flour.

Next, add the onion, bacon bits, chicken bouillon, garlic, ranch dressing, salt, parsley, and the pepper, and stir well.

Add the water to the slow cooker, and then place the lid on the slow cooker. Cook the potatoes on low for nine hours.

Next, add the half-and-half to the mixture. Stir, and cook for an additional 15 minutes.

Add cheddar cheese to the top of the soup, and serve warm.

Ground Beef "Hamburger" Stew

Recipe Makes 2 Servings.

Preparation Time: 8 hours and 20 minutes

Ingredients:

- ½ pound ground beef, lean
- ½ sliced potato, large
- ½ sliced celery stalk
- ½ tsp. salt
- ½ tsp. pepper
- ½ diced onion
- 7 ounces peas, canned
- 1 sliced carrot
- 5 ounces condensed tomato soup
- 1/3 cup water

Directions:

First, place ground beef in a large-sized skillet, and cook over medium-high heat until the ground beef is browned. Drain the ground beef skillet, crumble the ground beef, and then set the ground beef to the side.

Next, add the potatoes to the bottom of the slow cooker. Add the celery, then a layer of the ground beef. Salt and pepper the ground beef, and then add the carrots, onion, and the peas. Add the rest of the hamburger at this time.

To the side, stir together the water and the tomato soup, and then pour the mixture over the ground beef and vegetables.

Cover the mixture, and cook on low for eight hours. Serve warm, and enjoy.

Vegetarian's Delight Chili

Recipe Makes 2 Servings.

Preparation Time: 8 hours

Ingredients:

- 6 ounces black bean soup
- 4 ounces garbanzo beans, rinsed
- 4 ounces kidney beans, rinsed
- 3 ounces tomatoes, diced
- 4 ounces baked beans, vegetarian
- ½ diced onion
- 4 ounces corn
- 1/3 diced bell pepper
- ½ chopped celery stalk
- 1 minced garlic clove
- 1 tsp. chili powder
- 1 tsp. dried parsley
- 1 tsp. oregano
- 1 tsp. basil

Directions:

Add the bean soup, garbanzo beans, kidney beans, baked beans, corn, tomatoes, bell pepper, onion, and the celery to a slow cooker. Season with the spices, and stir well.

Cook the chili on high for two hours, or on low for eight hours. Stir well and serve warm.

Ham and Lentil Soup

Recipe Makes 4 Servings.

Preparation Time: 10 hours

Ingredients:

- 2/3 cup lentils, dried
- ½ cup chopped carrots
- 1 cup chopped celery
- 1 cup chopped onion
- 1 cup chopped ham, already cooked
- 3 minced garlic cloves
- ½ tsp. dried thyme
- ½ tsp. dried basil
- ½ tsp. oregano
- ½ tsp. pepper
- 1 bay leaf
- 1 cup water
- 3 cups chicken broth
- 1 tbsp. tomato sauce

Directions:

First, add the celery, lentils, onion, carrots, garlic, and the ham to a slow cooker. Stir well, and then add the spices: the bay leaf, thyme, basil, oregano, and pepper. Stir well, and then add the water, chicken broth, and the tomato sauce.

After giving the mixture a final stir, cover the slow cooker, and cook on low for ten hours. After ten hours, remove the bay leaf, and serve warm.

Wintertime Zucchini and Italian Sausage Soup

Recipe Makes 2 Servings.

Preparation Time: 6 hours and 20 minutes

Ingredients:

- 1 cup diced celery
- ½ pound Italian sausage, ground
- 14 ounces diced tomatoes
- 11 ounces diced zucchini
- 1/3 cup chopped onion
- ½ green pepper, sliced
- 1 tsp. salt
- 1/2 tsp. honey
- ¼ tsp. Italian seasoning
- ¼ tsp. dried basil
- ¼ tsp. garlic powder
- 2 tbsp. Parmesan, grated
- 1 cup chicken broth

Directions:

First, place a large skillet over medium-high heat, and then add the sausage to the skillet. Brown the sausage in the skillet until it crumbles and browns. This should take about seven minutes.

Drain the grease, and then add the celery to the sausage. Cook for an additional 10 minutes at this time, until the celery begins to soften.

Next, add the sausage, broth, celery, tomatoes, zucchini, green pepper, salt, onion, honey, and seasonings to a slow cooker. Stir well.

Place the lid on the slow cooker, and cook the soup on LOW for six hours. Serve warm, with Parmesan cheese on top, and enjoy.

:r's Best Chicken Noodle Soup

Recipe Makes 4 Servings

Preparation Time: 8 hours and 30 minutes

Ingredients:

- 3 boneless and skinless chicken breasts
- 4 cups chicken broth
- ½ diced onion
- 1 chopped celery stalk
- 1 tsp. salt
- 1 tsp. pepper
- 6 ounces egg noodles, frozen

Directions:

First, place the chicken, onion, celery, broth, pepper, and salt in the slow cooker. Stir well, and place the lid on the slow cooker. Cook the chicken on LOW for eight hours.

After eight hours, remove the chicken from the slow cooker and tear it using two forks. Place the chicken to the side, in a casserole dish, and ensure it stays warm.

At this time, elevate the slow cooker temperature to HIGH. Add the egg noodles. Cook the noodles in the slow cooker until they're tender—about 30 minutes—and then add the chicken to the slow cooker.

Salt and pepper to taste, and serve warm.

Mushroom and Chicken Stew

Recipe Makes 4 Servings

Preparation Time: 6 hours and 30 minutes

Ingredients:

- 1/3 cup flour
- 1 tsp. basil, dried
- 1 tsp. sage, dried
- 2 tsp. olive oil
- 4 chicken thighs, cut into bite-sized pieces
- ½ diced onion
- ½ diced green pepper
- 6 ounces chorizo sausage, sliced
- 1 cup chicken stock
- 5 ounces sliced mushrooms
- 5 ounces cream of mushroom soup, canned
- 1 cup sour cream
- 1 tsp. cayenne pepper

Directions:

First, stir together the basil, sage, and flour in a large, sealable bag. Add the chicken to the bag, seal the bag, and shake it to coat the chicken well.

Next, add the olive oil to a large skillet. Add the green pepper and the onion to the skillet, and cook for 10 minutes, stirring occasionally. Add the chorizo sausage, and stir and cook for an additional five minutes. At this time, pour the contents of the skillet into the slow cooker, and top it with the mushrooms.

Next, add the chicken, along with the ingredients of the bag, to the skillet. Brown the chicken for 10 minutes, making sure to flip it after five minutes.

Next, add the chicken stock to the skillet, and bring the mixture to a boil. After it begins to boil, scrape the bottom of the skillet, and transfer the chicken and the browned bottom bits to the slow cooker, along with the chicken stock.

Add the sour cream, mushroom soup, and the cayenne pepper to the slow cooker. Stir well, and cook the mixture on HIGH for two hours.

After two hours, reduce the slow cooker setting to LOW. Cook for an additional four hours, and serve warm.

SLOW COOKER SEAFOOD AND CHICKEN FOR TWO

Lime and Cilantro Chicken

Recipe Makes 4 Servings

Preparation Time: 4 hours

Ingredients:

- 8 ounces salsa
- ½ package taco seasoning mix
- 1 pound boneless and skinless chicken breasts
- 1 tbsp. cilantro, chopped
- Juice from ½ lime

Directions:

First, place the salsa, lime juice, taco seasoning, and the cilantro into the slow cooker, and stir well.

Next, add the chicken, and stir to coat the chicken well. Cover the slow cooker, and then set the slow cooker to high. Cook the chicken for four hours.

After four hours, shred the chicken with two forks, and serve warm.

Slow Cooked BBQ Chicken

Recipe Makes 2 Servings
Preparation Time: 8 hours

Ingredients:

- 2 chicken breasts, skinless and boneless
- 6 ounces BBQ sauce
- 1 tbsp. brown sugar
- 2 tbsp. Italian salad dressing
- 2 tsp. Worcestershire sauce

Directions:

First, add the chicken breasts to the slow cooker. To the side, stir together the salad dressing, BBQ sauce, Worcestershire sauce, and the brown sugar. Pour this mixture over the chicken.

At this time, place the lid on the slow cooker, and then cook on LOW for eight hours or on high for four hours.

At this time, shred the chicken with two forks, and serve warm, with more sauce over the chicken.

Southerner's Chicken Creole

Recipe Makes 4 Servings
Preparation Time: 12 hours

Ingredients:

- 4 chicken breasts, skinless and boneless
- 1 tsp. salt
- 1 tsp. pepper
- 1 tsp. Creole seasoning
- 1 diced celery stalk
- 14 ounces tomatoes, stewed, diced, with liquid
- 4 minced garlic cloves
- 1 diced green pepper
- 1 diced onion
- 5 ounces diced mushrooms
- 1 chopped jalapeno pepper

Directions:

First, place the chicken in the slow cooker, and salt and pepper the chicken. Add the Creole seasoning, and then add the rest of the ingredients: tomatoes, bell pepper, celery, onion, garlic, jalapeno peppers, and mushrooms.

Stir well, and place the lid on the slow cooker.

Cook the chicken on low for 12 hours or on high for six hours. Afterwards, shred the chicken with two forks, and serve warm.

Garlic and Honey Chicken

Recipe Makes 4 Servings
Preparation Time: 6 hours

Ingredients:

- 4 chicken thighs, skinless and boneless
- ½ cup soy sauce
- ½ cup honey
- 1/3 cup ketchup
- 4 minced garlic cloves
- 1 tsp. basil, dried

Directions:

First, place the chicken in the bottom of the slow cooker.

To the side, stir together the ketchup, soy sauce, honey, basil, and garlic in a small bowl. Pour the mixture over the chicken.

Place the lid on the slow cooker, and allow the chicken to cook on LOW for six hours.

Afterwards, serve the chicken warm, with extra sauce over it.

Asian Tang Chicken

Recipe Makes 2 Servings

Preparation Time: 9 hours

Ingredients:

- 9 ounces BBQ sauce
- 1/3 chopped green pepper
- 4 ounces pineapple chunks
- 1 minced garlic clove
- ¼ diced onion
- 2 skinless and boneless chicken breasts

Directions:

First, in a medium-sized bowl, stir together the pineapple, BBQ sauce, onion, bell pepper, and garlic.

Next, place the chicken at the bottom of the slow cooker. Pour the sauce over the chicken, making sure you coat it well.

Place the lid on the slow cooker, and cook the chicken on LOW for nine hours. Serve the chicken warm, and enjoy over rice or with a salad.

Chicken Adobo

Recipe Makes 4 Servings
Preparation Time: 8 hours

Ingredients:

- 1 diced onion
- 5 minced garlic cloves
- ½ cup soy sauce, low sodium
- 1.5 pounds chicken, diced into pieces
- 1/3 cup vinegar

Directions:

Add the chicken to the slow cooker.

To the side, stir together the onion, garlic, vinegar, and soy sauce, and pour this mixture over the chicken. Cook the chicken on low for eight hours.

After eight hours, serve the chicken warm, over rice if you like, with a bit of the sauce over top.

Italian Chicken Cacciatore

Recipe Makes 4 Servings

Preparation Time: 9 hours

Ingredients:

- 4 chicken breasts, boneless and skinless
- 12 ounces marinara sauce
- 1 cubed green pepper
- 5 ounces mushrooms, sliced
- ½ diced onion
- 1 tbsp. minced garlic

Directions:

First, place the chicken in the slow cooker. Add the marinara sauce, green pepper, mushrooms, onion, and garlic to the slow cooker, and then cover it.

Cook the chicken on LOW for nine hours, and serve warm. Enjoy.

Cheesy Cheddar Chicken

Recipe Makes 2 Servings
Preparation Time: 8 hours

Ingredients:

- 2 boneless and skinless chicken breasts
- ½ tsp. garlic powder
- 1 tsp. salt
- 1 tsp. pepper
- 5 ounces cream of chicken soup
- 5 ounces cream of mushroom soup
- 6 ounces cream of Cheddar cheese soup
- 4 ounces sour cream

Directions:

First, rinse off the chicken breasts, and pat them dry. Salt and pepper them, and then add garlic powder. Place the chicken in the slow cooker at this time.

Next, stir together the chicken soup, cream of mushroom soup, and the cream of cheddar cheese soup. Pour this mixture over the chicken.

Next, place the lid on the slow cooker, and cook the chicken on LOW for eight hours.

Just before serving, add the sour cream and stir. Serve the chicken warm.

African Marrakesh Chicken

Recipe Makes 4 Servings
Preparation Time: 5 hours

Ingredients:

- ½ diced onion
- 1 minced garlic clove
- 1 diced sweet potato
- 1 diced carrot
- 8 ounces garbanzo beans
- 1 pound boneless and chicken breasts, cubed
- ½ tsp. cumin
- ¼ tsp. turmeric
- ½ tsp. parsley
- ½ tsp. pepper
- ¼ tsp. cinnamon
- 1 tsp. salt
- 8 ounces diced tomatoes

Directions:

First, add the sweet potatoes, onion, garlic, carrots, garbanzo beans, and the chicken to the slow cooker.

To the side, stir together the spices, and then sprinkle the spices over the chicken and the vegetables.

Add the tomatoes to the mixture, and stir to combine them well.

Next, cover the slow cooker, set the slow cooker to HIGH, and then cook for five hours, or until the sauce is thick and the sweet potatoes are cooked all the way through. Serve warm, and enjoy.

South American Spiced Chicken

Recipe Makes 2 Servings

Preparation Time: 4 hours and 20 minutes

Ingredients:

- 1 pound chicken
- 1 tsp. olive oil
- 1 tbsp. cilantro, chopped
- 1 tsp. salt
- 1 tsp. pepper
- ½ diced red pepper
- ½ diced sweet potato
- 2 tbsp. chicken broth
- 8 ounces black beans
- ½ cup salsa
- ½ tsp. allspice, ground
- ½ tsp. cumin
- 1 minced garlic clove

Directions:

First, add olive oil to a skillet, and salt and pepper the chicken. Place the chicken in the skillet and brown it on all sides, for about three minutes on each side.

Next, place the chicken at the bottom of the slow cooker. Add the black beans, red pepper, and the sweet potatoes to the bottom of the slow cooker.

To the side, stir together the chicken broth, cilantro, salsa, allspice, cumin, and garlic. Then, pour this over the chicken and the vegetables.

Place the lid on the slow cooker, and turn the slow cooker on LOW.

Cook the chicken for four hours. Serve the chicken and vegetables warm, and enjoy.

Chicken from Thailand

Recipe Makes 2 Servings
Preparation Time: 5 hours and 30 minutes

Ingredients:

- 2 boneless and skinless chicken breasts, sliced into strips
- ½ diced onion
- ½ diced red pepper
- 1 tbsp. soy sauce
- 2 tbsp. chicken broth
- 1 tsp. cumin
- 1 minced garlic clove
- 2 tsp. cornstarch
- 1 tsp. salt
- 1 tsp. pepper
- ¼ tsp. red pepper flakes
- 3 tbsp. peanut butter
- 3 tbsp. chopped peanuts

Directions:

First, place the chicken the onion, and the bell pepper into the slow cooker.

Add the chicken broth and the soy sauce to the chicken mixture, followed with the spices and garlic. Stir well, and then cover the slow cooker. Cook the chicken on low for five hours.

Afterwards, remove ½ cup of the slow cooker's liquid, and stir this with the peanut butter, soy sauce, and the cornstarch. After it's fully combined, stir this mixture into the slow cooker, and then place the lid on the slow cooker.

Cook the chicken on high for an additional 30 minutes. Serve warm, with peanuts as garnish.

French Chicken Cooked with White Wine

Recipe Makes 4 Servings

Preparation Time: 8 hours

Ingredients:

- 4 skinless and boneless chicken breasts
- 1/3 cup dry white wine
- 1 tsp. salt
- 1 tsp. pepper
- 1 tsp. paprika
- 2 ounces sliced mushrooms
- 5 ounces cream of mushroom soup
- 1 cup sour cream
- 2 tbsp. flour

Directions:

First, salt, pepper, and paprika the chicken breasts. Place the chicken in the slow cooker.

To the side, stir together the canned soup, wine, and mushrooms. To the side, stir together the sour cream and the flour in another bowl. Next, add the sour cream and flour mixture to the mushroom mixture, and stir well.

Pour this mixture over the chicken. Place the lid on the slow cooker, and cook on LOW for eight hours. Serve warm, and enjoy.

Crab and Spinach Alfredo Lasagna

Recipe Makes 4 Servings

Preparation Time: 3 hours

Ingredients:

- 8 ounces Alfredo sauce
- ½ bunch chopped spinach
- 8 ounces dried lasagna noodles
- 7 sliced mushrooms
- 6 ounces cottage cheese
- 4 ounces crabmeat
- 6 ounces ricotta cheese
- 1 cup mozzarella cheese, shredded

Directions:

First, pour half of the Alfredo sauce into the slow cooker. Next, add a layer of lasagna noodles, followed by half of the spinach, mushrooms, and crabmeat.

Next, add half of the cottage cheese, followed by half of the ricotta cheese, and then repeat the layering until you run out of ingredients. Make sure that you end the layering with a layer of noodles and Alfredo sauce.

Next, place the lid on the slow cooker, and cook the lasagna on high for two hours and 20 minutes. Sprinkle the mozzarella cheese over the lasagna, and then cook on high for another 30 minutes. Serve the lasagna warm, and enjoy.

Salmon Casserole

Recipe Makes 4 Servings
Preparation Time: 3 hours

Ingredients:

- 2 cups water
- 1 cup white rice
- 12 ounces salmon
- 5 ounces cream of broccoli soup
- 5 ounces cream of chicken soup
- 2 tsp. dill weed
- 1 tsp. lemon pepper
- 1 cup peas, frozen

Directions:

First, add the salmon, water, rice, broccoli soup, chicken soup, dill, and the lemon pepper to the slow cooker, and stir well.

Place the lid on the slow cooker, and cook on high for two hours.

Next, add the peas to the mixture, and cook for an additional hour. At this time, serve the casserole warm, and enjoy.

South American Tilapia

Recipe Makes 4 Servings

Preparation Time: 2 hours and 40 minutes

Ingredients:

- 2 tbsp. lime juice
- 1 tsp. minced garlic
- 2 tsp. cumin
- 2 tsp. paprika
- 1 tsp. salt
- 1 tsp. pepper
- 1 pound tilapia, chopped
- 2 sliced bell peppers
- 1 diced onion
- 8 ounces diced tomatoes, drained
- 8 ounces coconut milk
- ½ bunch chopped cilantro

Directions:

First, stir together the cumin, lime juice, garlic, paprika, salt, and the pepper in a medium-sized bowl.

Add the tilapia to the bowl, and toss it well to coat. Cover the tilapia at this time, and allow it to marinate in the refrigerator for 30 minutes.

Next, add the tilapia, bell peppers, onion, tomatoes, and coconut milk to a slow cooker, stir well, and place the lid on the slow cooker. Cook the fish on HIGH for two hours.

After two hours, add the cilantro, and allow it to cook for 10 more minutes. Serve the fish warm, and enjoy.

SLOW COOKER BEEF AND PORK FOR TWO

Chicago's Favorite Italian Beef

Recipe Makes 4 Servings

Preparation Time: 1 hour and 10 minutes

Ingredients:

- 10 ounces sliced roast beef
- .4 ounces Italian-style salad dressing mix
- 5 ounces beef broth
- 8 ounces pepperoncini, sliced

Directions:

First, place the roast beef in the bottom of the slow cooker. Add the dressing mix, pepperoncini, and the beef broth.

Place the lid on the slow cooker, and cook on medium heat for one hour. Serve warm, and enjoy.

Cover the mixture with water, and then cover t slow cooker. Cook on high for four hours, or until the meat is tender.

At this time, remove the meat from the slow cooker. Pour out the liquid in the slow cooker, and then return the meat to the slow cooker. Shred it with two forks.

Next, add the tomato sauce, salt, and the chili powder to the slow cooker, and stir well.

Cover the slow cooker, and cook the meat for an additional two hours, on high. Serve warm, and enjoy.

.p Beef Loin Roast

Recipe Makes 4 Servings

.ration Time: 4 hours and 30 minutes

Ingredients:

- 1 pound beef loin tri-tip roast
- 2 tbsp. olive oil
- ½ beef bouillon cube
- 1/3 cup water
- ½ diced onion
- 1 minced garlic clove
- ½ pinch adobo seasoning

Directions:

First, add one tbsp. of olive oil to the bottom of the slow cooker, smearing it to coat.

Next, add the other tbsp. of olive oil to a skillet. Brown the beef on all sides in the skillet on medium-high heat. This should take about five minutes per side.

With five minutes remaining on the last side, add the onions.

Afterwards, add the beef to the slow cooker, keeping the onion in the skillet. Add water to the skillet, covering the onion, and then place the bouillon into the skillet. Add the garlic and the seasoning to the skillet, and cook for an additional five minutes, stirring occasionally.

At this time, pour the mixture over the beef in the slow cooker. Cover the slow cooker, and cook the beef on HIGH for four hours. Serve warm, and enjoy.

Eastern Asia Beef Tacos

Recipe Makes 2 Servings
Preparation Time: 8 hours

Ingredients:

- ¾ pound beef roast
- ¼ diced onion
- 2 tbsp. brown sugar
- 1 tbsp. soy sauce
- 2 minced garlic cloves
- ¼ diced jalapeno
- ¼ inch of ginger, diced
- 1 tsp. rice vinegar
- 1 tsp. sesame oil
- 1 tsp. salt
- 1 tsp. pepper

Lettuce wraps or corn tortillas to serve

Directions:

First, place the beef roast in the slow cooker. Add the brown sugar, onion, soy sauce, garlic, jalapeno, rice vinegar, ginger root, sesame oil, pepper, and salt. Stir well.

Next, place the lid on the slow cooker. Cook the beef on high for eight hours. After eight hours, shred the meat with two forks. Stir well, and then serve warm in lettuce wraps or corn tortillas.

Top Taste Beef Brisket

Recipe Makes 4 Servings

Preparation Time: 5 hours and 20 minutes

Ingredients:

- 2 tsp. paprika
- 2 tsp. garlic powder
- 2 tsp. salt
- 1 tsp. cayenne pepper
- 8 ounces sliced mushrooms
- 2 tbsp. olive oil
- 1 chopped shallot
- 1 tbsp. margarine
- 1 cup red wine
- 4 tbsp. water
- 2 pounds beef brisket
- 16 ounces beef broth
- 2 minced garlic cloves
- 2 tsp. Worcestershire sauce

Directions:

First, stir together the listed seasonings in a small bowl. Set this mixture of spices to the side at this time.

Add the olive oil to a skillet, and add the shallots and the mushrooms to the olive oil. Cook over medium-high heat for eight minutes. Set this mixture to the side.

Next, rub the beef with the spices. Add the margarine and the Worcestershire sauce to a large skillet, and then place the beef in the skillet. Heat over medium-high heat, and brown the beef on all sides. This should take about five minutes on each side.

Afterwards, place the brisket in the slow cooker. Add the red wine, water, beef broth, and garlic. Next, add the mushroom mixture.

Place the lid on the slow cooker, and cook on high for five hours. Afterwards, allow the brisket to rest for 15 minutes before slicing and serving.

Slow Cooked BBQ Beer Beef

Recipe Makes 4 Servings
Preparation Time: 10 hours and 30 minutes

Ingredients:

- ¼ diced onion
- 1 minced garlic clove
- 2 tbsp. white vinegar
- 2 tbsp. beer
- 1/3 cup ketchup
- 1 tsp. Worcestershire sauce
- 1 drop of liquid smoke flavoring
- ¼ tsp. salt
- ¼ tsp. chili powder
- ¼ tsp. paprika
- 2 tbsp. honey
- 1 pound beef brisket
- 1 tsp. water
- ½ tsp. cornstarch

Buns for serving, if you like

Directions:

First, place the onion and the garlic in the bottom of the slow cooker. Add the beer, ketchup, Worcestershire sauce, vinegar, and the liquid smoke.

Next, to the side in a small bowl, stir together the spices and the honey, until completely blended. Rub this mixture over the beef, and then place the beef in the slow cooker.

Next, place the lid on the slow cooker. Cook on LOW for 10 hours, or until the beef is easily shredded.

Next, remove the beef from the slow cooker. Remove the fat from the sauce in the slow cooker. Pour one cup of the slow cooker sauce into a saucepan, and bring this mixture to a simmer over medium heat.

Next, stir together the cornstarch and the water. Pour this mixture over the sauce. Stir well, cooking for an additional 10 minutes, until the sauce is thick. To the side, shred the meat with two forks.

Pour the sauce into a blender, and blend the mixture well. Add the sauce back to the slow cooker, followed by the beef, and stir it well. Serve the beef with the sauce over buns, or by itself.

Italian Pork Cacciatore

Recipe Makes 2 Servings

Preparation Time: 8 hours and 20 minutes

Ingredients:

- 1 tbsp. olive oil
- ½ diced onion
- 14 ounces pasta sauce
- 2 pork chops, boneless and skinless
- 14 ounces diced tomatoes
- ½ diced green pepper
- 1 minced garlic clove
- 4 ounces sliced mushrooms
- ½ tsp. basil
- ½ tsp. Italian seasoning
- 1/3 cup dry white wine

Directions:

First, place the pork chops in a large skillet over medium-high heat. Brown them on all sides, for about five minutes each side. At this time, place them in the slow cooker.

Next, add onion to the skillet, along with the olive oil. Cook until browned. Add the mushrooms and the bell pepper, and cook for five minutes, or until they're soft.

Add the pasta sauce, diced tomatoes, and the white wine to the skillet at this time. Add the spices, basil, and garlic.

At this time, pour the mixture over the pork chops in the slow cooker. Place the lid on the slow cooker, and cook the pork on LOW for eight hours.

Afterwards, serve the pork warm, covered in sauce.

Mexican Pork "Carnitas"

Recipe Makes 4 Servings

Preparation Time: 10 hours

Ingredients:

- ½ tsp. salt
- ½ tsp. cumin
- ½ tsp. garlic powder
- ¼ tsp. cinnamon
- ¼ tsp. coriander
- 2 pounds boneless pork shoulder
- 1 bay leaf
- 1 cup chicken broth

Directions:

Stir together the spices in a medium-sized bowl. Coat the pork shoulder with the spices, using your fingers to really dig into the meat.

Next, place the bay leaf at the bottom of the slow cooker. Add the pork to the slow cooker, and then pour the broth around the pork. Don't rinse off the spices.

Next, cover the slow cooker, and cook the pork on LOW until the pork shreds, or after approximately 10 hours. Ensure that you flip the meat over after five hours.

Afterwards, shred the pork, and serve warm.

Two-Ingredient Sauerkraut Pork

Recipe Makes 4 Servings

Preparation Time: 9 hours

Ingredients:

- 1½ pounds pork roast, boneless
- 7 ounces sauerkraut, drained

Directions:

First, place the pork roast on a cutting board. Slice a slit into the top of the pork, without going all the way through to the bottom.

Add the sauerkraut to the slit of the roast, pressing into it with a spoon to "fill" the inside.

Next, place the pork in the slow cooker. Place the lid on the slow cooker, and cook the meat on low for nine hours. Serve the pork warm, and enjoy.

Ultimate Tender Pork Roast

Recipe Makes 4 Servings
Preparation Time: 8 hours

Ingredients:

- 1 pound pork shoulder roast
- 1/3 cup soy sauce
- 4 ounces tomato sauce
- ¼ cup honey
- 1 tsp. mustard, ground

Directions:

First, position the pork roast into the slow cooker.

To the side, stir together the remainder of the ingredients: soy sauce, tomato sauce, honey, and the ground mustards. Pour this mixture over the roast, making sure you coat it well.

Place the lid on the slow cooker, and cook the pork for eight hours on LOW. Serve warm, and enjoy.

Super-Simple BBQ Pork

Recipe Makes 4 Servings

Preparation Time: 8 hours

Ingredients:

- 4 pork chops
- 20 ounces BBQ sauce
- 1 tsp. salt
- 1 tsp. pepper

Directions:

First, place the pork chops in the slow cooker.

Season the pork chops with salt and pepper. Pour the BBQ sauce over the pork chops, and mix the chops with the BBQ sauce using your hands to coat them well.

Cover the slow cooker, and cook on LOW for eight hours. Serve the pork chops warm, with extra BBQ sauce if you like.

Puerto Rican Pork

Recipe Makes 2 Servings
Preparation Time: 8 hours and 10 minutes

Ingredients:

- 1 minced garlic clove
- ½ diced onion
- 2 tsp. oregano, chopped
- 1 tsp. cumin
- 1 tsp. chili pepper
- 1 tsp. salt
- 1 tsp. pepper
- 1 tbsp. olive oil
- 1 tsp. white wine vinegar
- 1 pound pork loin roast, boneless

Directions:

First, add the garlic, onion, cumin, oregano, chili pepper, and salt and pepper to a food processor. Add the vinegar and the olive oil, and blend until smooth.

Add the pork to the slow cooker, and spread the sauce over the pork, making sure to coat it evenly.

Place the lid on the slow cooker, and cook the pork for eight hours on low. Afterwards, slice the pork into chunks and serve warm.

Super Picante Pork

Recipe Makes 4 Servings
Preparation Time: 9 hours

Ingredients:

- 1 ¼ pound pork tenderloin, cubed
- 4 ounces chopped green chilies
- 8 ounces hot picante sauce
- 4 ounces chipotle peppers in adobo sauce, canned
- Juice from one lime

Directions:

First, place the pork into the slow cooker. Add the picante sauce over the pork, followed by the chipotle peppers, green chilies, and lime juice.

Next, cover the slow cooker. Cook the pork on HIGH for five hours, or until you can shred the pork easily using two forks.

After five hours, shred the pork on a cutting board, and then return the pork to the slow cooker, where you can stir it with the sauce.

At this time, cook the pork in the sauce on low for an additional four hours. Serve warm, and enjoy.

SLOW COOKER VEGETARIAN RECIPES FOR TWO

Eggplant Parmesan for Two

Recipe Makes 2 Servings

Preparation Time: 5 hours and 40 minutes

Ingredients:

- 1 eggplant, peeled, sliced into ½ inch slices
- 1/3 cup olive oil
- 1 tsp. salt
- ½ egg
- 1 tbsp. water
- 2 tsp. all-purpose flour
- 1 tbsp. bread crumbs
- 2 tbsp. grated Parmesan cheese
- 8 ounces of marinara sauce
- 4 ounces sliced mozzarella cheese

Directions:

After preparing the eggplant, place the eggplant slices in a large bowl. Sprinkle each layer of eggplant with salt, and allow them to sit for 30 minutes. After 30 minutes, rinse the eggplant and allow them to dry on paper towels.

To the side, add olive oil to a skillet and heat over medium. Next, stir together the flour with the egg and the water. Stir until smooth.

Dip the slices of eggplant into the egg mixture, and then place them in the skillet. Fry them until golden.

To the side, stir together the parmesan cheese and the bread crumbs.

Add half of the eggplant slices to the bottom of the slow cooker. Add half of the bread crumbs over the eggplant, followed by half of the marinara sauce. Top this with a layer of mozzarella cheese. Next, repeat the layers.

Cover the slow cooker at this time, and cook on LOW for five hours. Afterwards, serve the eggplant warm, and enjoy.

Greek's Eggplant and Squash Stew

Recipe Makes 4 Servings
Preparation Time: 10 hours

Ingredients:

- ½ butternut squash, cubed and peeled
- 1 cup cubed eggplant, keep the peel
- 3 tbsp. vegetable broth
- 1 cup cubed zucchini
- 4 ounces tomato sauce
- 1 diced onion
- ½ diced tomato
- ½ diced carrot
- 2 tbsp. raisins
- 1 minced garlic clove
- ¼ tsp. crushed red pepper flakes
- ¼ tsp. turmeric
- ¼ tsp. cinnamon

Directions:

First, stir together the zucchini, butternut squash, tomato sauce, eggplant, tomato sauce, onion, tomato, carrot, vegetable broth, raisins, and garlic in a slow cooker. Add the spices, and stir well.

Place the lid on the slow cooker, and cook the stew on LOW for 10 hours. The vegetables should be tender and soft.

Slow Cooked Lentils and Barley

Recipe Makes 4 Servings

Preparation Time: 12 hours

Ingredients:

- 4 cups vegetable broth
- ½ ounce diced and dried shiitake mushrooms
- 1 cup sliced mushrooms, fresh
- 1/3 cup lentils, dried
- 1/3 cup pearl barley, uncooked
- 2 tbsp. dried onion flakes
- 1 tsp. minced garlic
- 1 bay leaf
- ½ tsp. basil, dried
- Salt and pepper to taste

Directions:

First, add the broth, mushrooms, shiitake mushrooms, lentils, barley, onion flakes, garlic, bay

Vegetarian Curry with Indian Spices

Recipe Makes 4 Servings
Preparation Time: 5 hours

Ingredients:

- 2 potatoes, cubed
- 2 tbsp. curry powder
- ½ red pepper, sliced
- 1 tbsp. flour
- ½ ounce dried onion soup mix
- 1 tsp. chili powder
- ¼ tsp. red pepper flakes
- ¼ tsp. cayenne pepper
- ½ sliced green pepper
- 7 ounces coconut cream, unsweetened
- 1 cup sliced carrots
- 2 tbsp. fresh cilantro, chopped, for garnish

Directions:

First, add the potatoes to the slow cooker.

To the side, stir together the flour, curry powder, chili powder, red pepper flakes, and cayenne pepper in a medium-sized bowl. Sprinkle this spice mixture over the potatoes. Stir well.

Next, add the peppers, onion soup mix, and coconut cream to the slow cooker. Stir well.

Cover the slow cooker.

Cook the mixture on LOW for four hours. As the mixture cooks, add water to keep the mixture moist.

At this time, add the carrots to the mixture. Cook for an additional 60 minutes.

Add the cilantro for garnish, and serve the meal warm.

Parsnip, Turnip and Carrot Tagine

Recipe Makes 4 Servings
Preparation Time: 9 hours

Ingredients:

- ½ pound peeled and diced parsnips
- 1 diced onion
- ½ pound peeled and diced turnips
- ½ pound diced and peeled carrots
- 3 chopped apricots, dried
- ½ tsp. turmeric
- 2 chopped prunes
- ¼ tsp. ginger
- ¼ tsp. cinnamon
- 1 tsp. dried parsley
- 1 tsp. dried cilantro
- 7 ounces vegetable broth

Directions:

Add the parsnips, onion, turnips, carrots, apricots, turmeric, prunes, ginger, cinnamon, parsley, cilantro, and the broth to the slow cooker.

Place the lid on the slow cooker, and cook the mixture on low for nine hours. Serve warm, and enjoy.

Spinach and Pumpkin Chili

Recipe Makes 4 Servings
Preparation Time: 4 hours and 30 minutes

Ingredients:

14 ounces diced tomatoes

7 ounces pure pumpkin puree

1/3 cup vegetable juice

1/3 cup chopped okra

1/3 cup chopped broccoli

1 tbsp. sugar

½ diced zucchini

½ diced onion

2 tsp. pumpkin pie spice

½ tsp. chili powder

½ tsp. salt

9 ounces fava beans

1 cup chopped spinach

2 tsp. white vinegar

Directions:

First, add the tomatoes, pumpkin, okra, vegetable juice, sugar, broccoli, carrot, zucchini, onion, pumpkin pie spice, vinegar, chili powder, pepper, and salt to the slow cooker. Cook the chili on HIGH for four hours.

Afterwards, stir in the spinach and the fava beans. Cook for another 30 minutes on HIGH. Serve warm, and enjoy.

Veggie-Friendly Buffalo Dip

Recipe Makes 4 Servings

Preparation Time: 2 hours and 10 minutes

Ingredients:

- 8 ounces chicken-style vegetarian strips, diced
- 16 ounces low-fat ranch salad dressing
- 16 ounces cream cheese, softened
- 12 ounces hot sauce
- 1 cup Colby Jack cheese, shredded

Directions:

First, add the fake chicken strips, cream cheese, hot sauce, and the ranch dressing to the slow cooker. Stir well, and heat on LOW for two hours.

After two hours, add the shredded cheese to the mixture. Stir well, and serve warm.

Cheesy and Buttery Squash

Recipe Makes 4 Servings

Preparation Time: 1 hour and 10 minutes

Ingredients:

- 1 pound summer squash, sliced
- ½ diced onion
- 1 tbsp. butter, cubed
- 1 ½ ounces American cheese, cubed

Directions:

First, add the squash and the onion to a saucepan. Add enough water to cover the two ingredients, and bring the mixture to a boil.

Cover the pot and allow the vegetables to simmer for 10 minutes. Don't stir the vegetables during this time.

Afterwards, drain the vegetables, and add them in the bottom of the slow cooker. Add the butter and the American cheese, and give the mixture a final stir.

Place the lid on the slow cooker, and cook the squash on LOW for one hour. Don't stir during this time. Serve the squash warm, and enjoy.

Split Black Lentils with Curry

Recipe Makes 4 Servings
Preparation Time: 5 hours

Ingredients:

- 3 cups water
- 1 cup split black lentils
- 1 minced garlic clove
- ¼ chopped onion
- 1 tsp. sugar
- ½ tsp. turmeric powder
- 1 tsp. curry powder
- 1/3 cup heavy cream
- ½ inch of fresh ginger
- Salt to taste

Directions:

First, add the water, onion, lentils, garlic, salt, sugar, curry powder, ginger root, and turmeric to the slow cooker. Stir well.

Place the lid on the slow cooker, and cook on HIGH for five hours. At this time, add the cream to the slow cooker, stir until well combined, and serve warm.

Rice and Mushroom Casserole

Recipe Makes 4 Servings

Preparation Time: 10 hours

Ingredients:

- 1 diced onion
- 1 sliced celery stalk
- 6 ounces long grain rice, dry
- 1 cup water
- 5 ounces cream of mushroom soup, condensed
- ¼ cup butter
- ¼ pound American cheese, cubed
- 1/3 cup sliced mushrooms

Directions:

Add the onion, celery, long grain rice, water, cream of mushroom soup, butter, American cheese, and the sliced mushrooms to the slow cooker.

Cover the mixture and cook on LOW for 10 hours. Stir well, and serve the mixture warm.

Slow Cooked Artichoke Dip

Recipe Makes 4 Servings

Preparation Time: 2 hours and 20 minutes

Ingredients:

- 2 tsp. olive oil
- 1 tsp. butter
- ½ diced onion
- 2 tsp. flour
- 1 minced garlic clove
- ½ diced red pepper
- 2 tbsp. dry white wine
- 2 tbsp. half-and-half
- 1/3 cup vegetable broth
- 5 ounces artichoke hearts
- 1 cup shredded mozzarella cheese

Directions:

First, pour the olive oil and the butter into a medium-sized pan. Add the garlic, red pepper, and the onion to the pan, and cook for five minutes, or until the onion is transparent.

At this time, add the flour to the mixture. Stir well, and then add the dry white wine. Bring the mixture to a simmer, and then pour the mixture into the slow cooker.

Add the vegetable broth to the mixture, followed by the artichoke hearts. Place the lid on the slow cooker, and cook on LOW for two hours. Add the half-and-half to the mixture, along with the mozzarella cheese, and stir well until the cheese is completely melted.

Serve the artichoke dip warm, and enjoy.

Vegetarian Minestrone

Recipe Makes 4 Servings

Preparation Time: 8 hours

Ingredients:

- 3 cups vegetable broth
- 7 ounces kidney beans
- 14 ounces crushed tomatoes
- ½ diced onion
- 1 diced celery stalk
- 1 diced carrot
- ½ cup green beans
- ½ zucchini, diced
- 2 minced garlic cloves
- 2 cups spinach
- 1/3 cup elbow macaroni
- 1 tsp. minced parsley
- 1 tsp. dried oregano
- 1 tsp. salt
- 2 tbsp. grated Parmesan cheese

Directions:

Add the broth, kidney beans, tomatoes, celery, onion, green beans, carrots, garlic, zucchini, and the spices to the slow cooker. Stir well.

Place the lid on the slow cooker and cook on LOW for eight hours.

To the side, bring a large pot of water to a boil. Add the macaroni to the water, and allow it to cook for about eight minutes, or until it's cooked through, but firm. Drain the macaroni at this time.

Next, add the macaroni and the spinach to the slow cooker. Place the lid back on the slow cooker, and cook for an additional 15 minutes.

Stir well, and add the Parmesan cheese. Serve warm, and enjoy.

Vegan Jambalaya

Recipe Makes 4 Servings
Preparation Time: 3 hours and 20 minutes

Ingredients:

- 10 ounces cream-style corn
- 13 ounces corn
- 4 ounces frozen and pre-diced hash brown potatoes
- 1 tsp. butter
- ½ diced onion
- ½ diced red onion
- 1 diced green pepper
- 1 chopped celery stalk
- 1 diced carrot
- ½ diced jalapeno pepper
- 1 diced Poblano pepper
- 1 cup half-and-half

Directions:

Add the cream corn and the regular corn to the slow cooker. Heat the slow cooker on LOW at this time, and then add the hash browns. Stir well.

To the side, place the butter in a skillet over medium. Add the red and regular onion, the bell pepper, celery, carrot, jalapeno pepper, and Poblano pepper. Cook until the onions are see-through, which should take about 10 minutes.

Afterwards, add the vegetable mixture to the slow cooker. Add half-and-half to the top of the vegetables.

Place the lid on the slow cooker, and cook on LOW for three hours. Stir occasionally.

Serve warm, and enjoy.

SLOW COOKER DESSERT RECIPES FOR TWO

Pumpkin Pie Spiced Apple Sauce

Recipe Makes 4 Servings
Preparation Time: 8 hours and 30 minutes

Ingredients:

- 4 cored, peeled, and sliced apples
- 1/3 cup water
- 1/3 cup brown sugar, packed
- ¼ tsp. pumpkin pie spice

Directions:

First, add the apples and the water to the slow cooker. Cook the apples on LOW for eight hours.

After eight hours, add the brown sugar and the pumpkin pie spice to the slow cooker. Cook for an additional 30 minutes. Stir well, and serve either warm or cold.

Slow Cooked Tapioca Pudding

Recipe Makes 2 Servings

Preparation Time: 3 hours or 6 hours

Ingredients:

- 1 cup milk
- 2 tbsp. white sugar
- ½ egg
- 2 tbsp. small pearl tapioca

Directions:

First, stir together the milk, egg, sugar, and tapioca in a slow cooker.

Cover the slow cooker, and cook on medium heat for three hours, or for six hours on the lowest setting. Stir occasionally as it cooks.

Serve the tapioca pudding warm, and enjoy.

Grandma's Best Chocolate Cake

Recipe Makes 4 Servings

Preparation Time: 3 hours and 40 minutes

Ingredients:

- 2/3 cup white sugar
- ¼ cup cocoa powder
- ½ cup all-purpose flour
- ½ tsp. baking soda
- ½ tsp. baking powder
- ½ egg
- ¼ tsp. salt
- 2 tbsp. olive oil
- 1/3 cup milk
- 1/3 cup water, boiling
- 2 tsp. vanilla

Directions:

First, spray the bottom of the slow cooker with a cooking spray of your choice.

Next, to the side, stir together the sugar, cocoa, flour, baking soda, baking powder, and the salt in a medium-sized bowl.

In a smaller bowl, stir together the vanilla, oil, milk, water and egg until totally combined. Add the wet ingredients to the flour mixture, and stir well.

Pour this mixture into the slow cooker, and then set the slow cooker to the lowest setting.

Cook for about three hours on LOW. After three hours, allow the cake to rest for about 40 minutes. Serve at this time, and enjoy.

Peach Cobbler

Recipe Makes 4 Servings
Preparation Time: 4 hours and 10 minutes

Ingredients:

- ½ cup oats, old-fashioned
- ½ cup sugar
- 1/3 cup brown sugar
- ½ tsp. cinnamon
- 1/3 cup Bisquick baking mix
- 4 fresh peaches, pitted, peeled and sliced

Directions:

First, spray the inside of your slow cooker to avoid sticking.

Next, stir together the white sugar, oats, brown sugar, baking mix, and cinnamon in a large-sized bowl. Add the peaches, stir, and then pour the mixture into the slow cooker.

Place the lid on the slow cooker, and cook on LOW for four hours. Serve warm, and enjoy.

Conclusion

The Slow Cooker Cookbook for Two is the extensive recipe book for those on-the-go, empty nesters, or busy professionals who just don't have the time, resources, or inclination to make 8- or 10-serving recipes any longer. With this book, which is filled with countless, nutritional, vegetable and meat-based meals, you can lose weight, rev your metabolism, and finally save some much-needed time.

Toss the ingredients in the slow cooker. Follow the simple instructions—often just "flip the switch to the lowest setting"—and forget about your meal until you're hungry enough to eat it. Then, do it all over again the next day, with a different recipe. Your life is about to get much, much easier. Trust me.

Made in the USA
Lexington, KY
24 January 2018